YOUR KNOWLEDGE HAS VALUE

AF153456

Review of Gender Roles in Community Management of Forest Resources. A Case of Nandi, Uasin Gishu and Elgeyo Marakwet Counties

Brian Ambale

Bibliographic information published by the German National Library:

The German National Library lists this publication in the National Bibliography; detailed bibliographic data are available on the Internet at http://dnb.dnb.de.

ISBN: 9783346653369
This book is also available as an ebook.

Print and binding: Books on Demand GmbH, Norderstedt, Germany
Printed on acid-free paper from responsible sources.

The present work has been carefully prepared. Nevertheless, authors and publishers do not incur liability for the correctness of information, notes, links and advice as well as any printing errors.

GRIN web shop: https://www.grin.com/document/1220651

A Review of Gender Roles in Community Management of Forest Resources: A Case of Nandi, Uasin Gishu and Elgeyo Marakwet Counties

Brian Ambale

SES 983: COMPARATIVE ANALYSIS OF GENDER IN MANAGEMENT OF RESOURCES

Abstract

This paper reviews gender roles in community management of forests across three counties in Kenya namely: Nandi, Uasin Gishu, and Elgeyo Marakwet Counties. It seeks to establish an equilibrium in analyzing the access, use, and management of forest resources by individuals from both sides of the gender divide. This paper primarily investigates the relevant secondary data in line with the operationalization of the theme. It also suggests that these differences may be related to three factors: gender equity in access and dissemination of technology, a labor constraint faced by women, and a possible limitation to women's sanctioning authority. Mixed female and male groups offer an avenue for exploiting the strengths of women and men while tempering their shortcomings.

Keywords: Gender roles; forest cover; deforestation; conservation; water catchments.

Contents

1. INTRODUCTION

Forests are complex ecological systems where trees are the supreme life form (Britannica, 2022). Both the "land cover" and land use" schools of thought attempt to explain fundamentally what forests are. From the "land cover" viewpoint, forests are regarded as ecosystems or vegetation types supporting exceptional collections of flora and fauna (Chazdon et al., 2016). Nevertheless, Chazdon et al. (2016) also mention that the "land use" standpoint sees forests as landholdings lawfully chosen as forests, irrespective of their existing vegetation. There are three main types of forests, defined by latitude: taiga (boreal) forests, temperate forests, and tropical forests (Britannica, 2022). The global forest cover is at 31 percent of the land area (FAO, 2022b). Forests play numerous responsibilities in the climate context by serving as carbon sinks, water regulation, supporting agriculture, and providing livelihoods and energy sources for women and men (Marin & Kuriakose, 2017). Projections show that natural resources such as forests necessary to sustain the human population will in the future surpass existing resources at the then-current consumption levels (Phiri et al., 2022).

Gender equity is important in the context of prudent management, use, and access of forest resources. In the broadest terms possible, gender equity, therefore, refers to the impartiality and justice in delivering benefits and responsibilities amongst men and women (WHO, 2022). Men and women possess diverse spaces in which they have authority. Responsibilities and freedoms are necessary for understanding these roles for agroforestry research and development beneficial to both men and women (Kiptot, 2015). Gender roles are the activities that both men and women display in private and public domains (Tong, 2012). The expectations of these roles might impact underachievement and creativity (Kim & Zabelina, 2011). In the context of specialized forestry, there has been a mounting appreciation that gender roles, knowledge, and interests have been under-acknowledged (Colfer, 2013).

In communities dependent on forests for their livelihoods, gender relations can affect access to forest resources, income, and food generating activities (Chiwona-Karltun et

3

al., 2017). Subsequently, Chiwona-Karltun et al. (2017) explain that gender-mediated access to forest products might lead to diverse food security results for men, women, and children. Men are often the sole decision-makers on issues about the conservation of forest resources, which hampers the implementation of forest conservation measures (Koech, 2020). Studies show that women rely more seriously on direct access to forest resources as they are accountable for day-to-day domestic work, which includes finding food and fetching firewood, as their husbands are fixated on work off-farm [(Nhem & Lee, 2019); (Ros-Tonen et al., 2018); (Das, 2011)]. Women comprise a substantial percentage of the labor force in forest industries, particularly in tree nursery work and in events extending from wood processing to logging (FAO, 2022a).

A forest in Kenya, as defined by the National Forest Programme (NFP, 2016-2020), refers to a piece of land of more than half a hectare (0.5ha), with a tree canopy cover of above 10% and trees of at best two and a half meters (2.5m) height while the land is not principally under agricultural or other specific non-forest land use (Schnell et al., 2015). The types of forest ecosystems in Kenya include savannah woodlands, dry forests, mountain rainforests, coastal forests, and mangroves (Peltorinne, 2004). Some of the forests in Kenya include Kankamega forest, Karura forest, Mau forest, Boni forest, Menengai forest, Kaya forest, Cherangani forest, Ruri Hills forest, God Oogo forest, Got Okombo forest (E. Centre, 2020). Mount Kenya plays a critical role in water catchment for Kenya. It is one of the five main water towers in the country, with Aberdare Range, Mau Complex, Cherangani Hills, and Mount Elgon all providing most of the country's water (Forest, 2021).

Approximately 3,467,000 ha of Kenya is forested (Cheboiwo et al., 2018). Kenya's forests contain approximately 476,000,000 metric tons of carbon in living forest biomass (Mongabay, 2021). Mountain forests play an irreplaceable role in water catchment, retaining and releasing water in the hydrological cycle (Morara & Kiptoo, 2018). Morara and Kiptoo noted that the highland forest cover causes clouds that form precipitation. However, the forest cover in Kenya has declined due to human demand. Kenya lost roughly 12,050 ha or 0.32% per year between 1990 and 2010 (Mongabay, 2021). The forest cover in Kenya stands at 7.4%, 3.6% short of the constitutional requirement of 10% forest cover (NEMA, 2022).

2. LITERATURE

2.1 Legal Frameworks and Constitutional Requirements

Sustainable forest development typically refers to recognizing the ability and limits of forests to endure environmental change, independently and together, and in dealing with human activities to produce the supreme level of benefits attainable in these bounds (Maini, 1992). Sustainable Development Goal 15 seeks to restore, protect, and encourage sustainable use of terrestrial ecosystems, sustainably manage forests, fight desertification, stop and reverse land degradation and break the cyclic loss of biodiversity (UN, 2022). The agenda also discusses the significance of refining human, practical and specialized skills, along with knowledge and proficiencies the efficient formulation and implementation of policies, strategies, programs, research, and projects on management, conservation, and sustainable development of all types of forests and forest-based resources, and forest lands, as well as other areas from which forest benefits can be derived (UN, 2022).

Deforestation is the deliberate cutting down of trees in forested lands (Society, 2019). The environmental impacts of illicit logging consist of greenhouse gas emissions, deforestation, and the loss of biodiversity (FLEGT, 2022). According to Society (2019), forests have been destroyed to create space for meadows (meant for animal grazing) and agriculture, and for the acquisition of wood fuel, construction, and industrialization throughout history and in recent days. Unlawful logging contributes to conflicts with local populations, violence, human rights abuses, corruption, funding of armed conflicts, and the worsening of poverty (FLEGT, 2022). Stopping deforestation is one of the best ways to conserve and protect wildlife and secure the rights of communities that are reliant on forests. The United States of America (U.S.) has in place laws like the

5

Wilderness Act, the Endangered Species Act, the Roadless Rule, and the Lacey Act to support the protection of forests and to put an end to banned wood products against penetrating the U.S. markets (Greenpeace, 2022). Likewise, in Kenya, the Forest Conservation and Management Act of 2016 states that any individual that deliberately or maliciously sets fire to any public, provisional, community, or private forest commits a crime and is liable on conviction to a fine not more than a hundred thousand Kenya shillings or imprisonment for a term not below a year, or both such fine and imprisonment (FCMA, 2016).

Article 69(1)(b) of the Kenyan constitution necessitates the Country to intensify and uphold a tree cover of at least 10% of the total land area (L. O. Kenya, 2013). The Kenya Vision 2030 sets the environmental sector as a social pillar. This document (the Kenya Vision 2030) highlights the need to conserve natural resources such as forests to sustain economic growth (Kenya. Ministry of Planning and National Development & Kenya. National Economic and Social Council, 2007). In the Medium Term Plan III, the Kenyan government committed itself to protect natural forests in the water towers and their continuous rehabilitation of landscapes to increase and sustain water flow and ecological integrity (T. Kenya, 2013). This is strengthened in section 6(3)(a)(iii) of the Forest Conservation and Management Act 2016 (FCMA – 2016), which describes the requirement necessary for developing critical programs to achieve and maintain tree cover of at least 10% of Kenya's land area (FCMA, 2016). FCMA (2016) further elaborately requires every County Government in section 37(1) to create and sustain functioning arboreta, green zones, or leisure parks for residents within their area of jurisdiction.

Article 27(8) of the Kenyan constitution states that the State shall take measures to ensure that not more than two-thirds of members of all appointive and elective positions are not of a similar gender (L. O. Kenya, 2013). However, since the promulgation of the currently operational Kenyan constitution, specific legislation to operationalize gender equity has not yet been enacted. Both levels of the Kenyan

Parliament (the Senate and the National Assembly) have been criticized for failing to enact pertinent legislation touching on the two-thirds gender principle. The absence of the necessary legislation to strengthen the two-thirds gender principle has subsequently negatively affected the gradual full management of natural resources such as forests within the country. Section 6(4) of FCMA – 2016 is the only section of the Act that talks about the observation of either the principle of gender or regional representation in the appointment of the members of the Forests Board (FCMA, 2016). This is a serious limitation since it does not trickle down to lower levels as far as forest management, access and use are concerned.

Both section 9(2)(r) and Section 44 of the Environmental Management and Coordination CAP 387 and (Amendment) Act of 2015 (EMCA-2015) obligates National Environment Management Authority (NEMA) and other lead agencies to protect forests and conduct environmental impact assessments of forest-related developments (EMCA, 2015). Despite the robustness in the Kenyan legal framework in all its spheres (both at the national and the county level), there is still an overwhelming inadequacy in the jurisprudence regarding gender equity as far as forest resource use and management is involved. Therefore, women should be incorporated into the decision-making process (Koech, 2020) and through the complete access and control of forest resources at both the national and county level.

2.2 Forest Use, Access, and Management

Forest management is the method of planning and implementing practices for the stewardship and use of forests to meet precise environmental, economic, social, and cultural aims (FAO, 2020). FAO (2020) explains that forest management deals with the administrative, economic, legal, social, technical, and scientific aspects of managing natural and planted forests. The commercial, socio-cultural, legal, and political backgrounds can influence the rights of both men and women to regulate forest resources and land ownership (FAO, 2022a). Sustainable forestry is a practice that can protect or encourage forest regeneration, including putting up fences, controlling weeds and other evasive plants, and removing some trees to allow more sunlight to reach down into the forest (Jacobson & Smith, 2016).

The role of women in forest resources management is vital. Collection of forest products to meet subsistence requirements and augment the family's income is generally the responsibility of women (Jattan, 2003). Against contrary beliefs, women often have exceedingly specific knowledge of trees and forests in terms of management, species diversity, conservation, and use (FAO, 2022a). However, gender inequality brings about hindrances to effective, sustainable development and livelihoods by preventing or confining women's right to access essential resources and decision-making opportunities (GEN, 2022). Women participate in the forest sector in several ways, both formal and informal, not excluding forest protection, watershed management, tree improvement, and agroforestry (FAO, 2022a).

Forest ecosystems provide food, fuel, and fiber and aid in air purification, filtration of water supplies, flood and erosion control, sustain genetic resources and biodiversity, and provide prospects for education, recreation, and cultural improvement (Millennium ecosystem assessment, 2005). The main goal for forest management is better for the environment and the well-being of the forest than conventional logging methods (LLC, 2017). A common generalization is that forests are vital for the underprivileged, who often happen to be women, and who more than often do not own parcels of land but use resources from forests for subsistence, as safety nets, and even earn a basic income (Koech, 2020). Women are frequently excluded from participation for several reasons, including; the guidelines governing the community forestry groups, social barriers emanating from cultural constructs of gender responsibilities, roles and expected behavior, logistical barricades connecting the length and timings of institutional meetings, and male prejudice in the attitudes of those sponsoring community forestry initiatives (Mwangi et al., 2011).

2.3 Benefits of Forests

Forests around the world have immense benefits to the environment. Apart from helping maintain the nutrient cycle, they stabilize the soil, hence they help minimize erosion and reduce the decline in water quality due to sedimentation (PEFC, 2022). According to PEFC (2022), woodlands shield watercourses and water bodies by trapping sediments and pollutants from additional up-slope land uses and activities while serving as a safeguard in natural catastrophes such as floods. They also assist in the reduction of the dangers of air pollution, aid in rainwater filtration, as well as the provision of shade under the scorching sun during hot days (Oregon Forest Resources Institute, 2022).

Globally, forests provide fresh air, clean water, timber and act as carbon sinks (Oregon Forest Resources Institute, 2022). Besides providing livelihoods for millions of people, they also offer food, medicine, habitat, and biodiversity for wildlife (IFPC, 2022), and other goods such as timber, fuel, in addition to other bioproducts necessary for either domestic or industrial human consumption (Canada, 2017). It is also worth noting that forests have social and cultural benefits like spirituality, traditional resource uses, and recreation (Canada, 2017). In Kenya, some of the forests that are considered by local communities as sacred include Ramogi Hills Forest Reserve (found on the northeastern shores of Lake Victoria basin) and the Mijikenda Kaya Forest (found along Kenya's coastal region) [(Sigu et al., 2000); (U. W. H. Centre, 2022)]. Trees and other plants in forests provide most of the oxygen through a process called photosynthesis which is essential to all aspects of life on earth (Oregon Forest Resources Institute, 2022).

Many forests act as a watershed (commonly referred to as "water catchment"). A watershed is an area of land where all water flows to one stream, river, lake, or even ocean (Alliance, 2022). A vibrant watershed not only offers high-quality drinking water and supports livelihoods (like agriculture, water sports, and recreational angling), but also supports local ecosystems so plants, animals, fish, and insects that rely on the water can bloom and flourish (Catchments, 2022). The five main forest water catchment areas in Kenya are Aberdares Ranges Forest, Cherangani Hills Forest, Mau Forest Complex, Mount Elgon Forest, and Mount Kenya Forest (Forest, 2021).

3. GENDER ROLES IN THE MANAGEMENT OF FORESTS

There is a looming conflict between agriculture and closed-canopy forests for these forests exist in the zones most appropriate for numerous crops like maize (Chebii, 2015). According to Chebii (2015), most of the potential forest areas have been cleared of natural vegetation and converted to agricultural land. This has led to the gradual rise of agroforestry within the country (Kenya). Agroforestry offers significant benefits to women; nevertheless, their contribution is low in initiatives that are deemed as men's field, for example, timber harvesting, and high in enterprises that have little or no marketable cost, like gathering of indigenous fruits and vegetables (Kiptot & Franzel, 2012).

Agroforestry is a collective term for land-use systems and technologies where woody perennials (trees, shrubs, palms, bamboos, etc.) are intentionally used on the same land-management units as crops and/or animals, in some form of spatial arrangement or temporal sequence (FAO, 2015). It is more than just mixing crops and trees though. It's farming in places like in and along the edges of forests, which previously wouldn't have been done (GroCycle, 2022). The degree of women's involvement relative to men in technologies such as soil fertility management, fodder production, and woodlots is fairly high in terms of the proportion of female-headed households participating but is low as measured by the area they allocate to these activities and the number of trees they plant (Kiptot & Franzel, 2012).

3.1 Forests in Nandi County

The Nandi forests are generally considered indigenous forests (Kagombe, 2015). The Nandi forest ecosystem mainly encompasses Kaptorio, Nandi North, Nandi South (a tropical rain forest which also happens to be the largest forest cover in the county as per the Nandi County Integrated Development Plan 2018-2023 (County Government of

10

Nandi, 2018)), Ururu, and Taressia forest blocks (ISSUU, 2015). The forests in this county are key water catchments for Lake Victoria (Tanui & Saina, 2015). Recently, Nandi County enacted an ambitious piece of legislation (the Nandi County Wetlands Conservation and Management Policy Act of 2021) to help it attain a 30% forest cover milestone up from its present 26.2% the year 2030 (Daily, 2021). Nevertheless, studies show that the Nandi Hills and forest faced substantial deterioration and degradation in recent times, thereby impacting the hydrological quality and quantity in the Lake Victoria Basin (Tanui & Saina, 2015). There are no defined areas for community utilization, so residents let their livestock graze freely and collect firewood anywhere within these forests (Kagombe, 2015). Kagombe (2015) states that a management plan exists in Nandi County that envisages delineating the belt adjacent to settlement areas as a utilization zone and marking some sites as seasonal grazing areas, especially the natural grazing land. The uptake of on-farm forestry by the residents of this county is seen as a potential remedy for the dwindling forest cover (Tanui & Saina, 2015).

The essential forest products in Nandi County are timber, poles, grass, wood fuel (which is used in tea factories and domestically), herbs, and medicines (County Government of Nandi, 2018). High levels of poverty and unemployment among the residents (especially among women) influence the encroachment of forests in the county. South Nandi forest, for instance, is a good source of firewood and the most common source of fuel available to the local community (Koech, 2020). Forest fires, charcoal burning, and logging are the main challenges impeding forest conservation in this county. Charcoal burning, for instance, is a crucial problem done commercially. Essentially, women sell the charcoal in tins around marketplaces, while men are primarily involved in extracting timber (Koech, 2020). According to Koech (2020), some communities in Nandi County do not allow women to plant trees, which is worsened by men owning most of the land (yet women need forests more than their male counterparts, particularly for the provision of firewood (Fashing et al., 2004)). The main threats to Nandi County's Forest ecosystem are deforestation and overgrazing.

11

According to County (2018), deforestation has been the major environmental threat and is caused by both commercial and illegal logging in addition to forest encroachment. Overgrazing has also brought about the destruction of natural vegetation, which has additionally aided in soil erosion, particularly in the rainy season (County Government of Nandi, 2018).

3.2 Forests in Uasin Gishu County

With a total of 29,802 hectares of gazetted forests, Uasin Gishu county has 13,184 hectares (44% of her forest cover) under plantation, whereas 16,618 ha (56%) are categorized as indigenous forest [(County Government of Uasin Gishu, 2018); (Rutto & Odhiambo, 2017)]. The gazetted forests in this county include Kapsaret, Timboroa (which forms part of Kenya's five water towers (Daily, 2020)), Lurenge, Kipkurere, Nabkoi, and Singalo [(County Government of Uasin Gishu, 2018); (County, 2013)]. From 2001 to 2020, Uasin Gishu County lost approximately 11.7 kilo-hectares of tree cover, similar to a 33% reduction since 2000 (Vizzuality, 2022). The over-dependence on trees for fuel; and the use of wetlands for agricultural practices have resulted in deforestation and encroachment on river banks (County Government of Uasin Gishu, 2018).

Both County (2013) and County Government of Uasin Gishu (2018) noted that deforestation had, on its part, led to erratic weather conditions, thus significantly affecting agriculture. In an attempt to boost environmental conservation and achieve 10% forest cover in the county, Uasin Gishu County had strategies of planting Bamboo (KNA, 2019). In 2018, however, members of the Indian community also planted more than 23,000 trees on a 4.6 hectares piece of land in Uasin Gishu County's Timboroa forest to intensify forest cover as part of an afforestation program (Daily, 2020). A vast market for timber, poles, and wood fuel exists within and outside the county. The high demand for softwood sawn timber, primarily cypress (*C. Lusitanica*), has brought about a steady increase in the planting of woodlots in the county (County Government of Uasin Gishu, 2018).

The focal drivers of dilapidation in Kenya's upper catchment areas consist of the growth of agriculture, harvesting of wood fuel, both legal and illegal logging, poor implementation of forest protection laws and regulation, forest excision for settlements, invasive alien flora and fauna species, quick urbanization, rising demand for timber and charcoal trade, and other forms of human encroachment (King-Okumu et al., 2021). Studies show that the rate at which trees are being cut down in Uasin Gishu County is higher than the replanting rate (County Government of Uasin Gishu, 2018). It is mainly because of encroachment on restricted areas like road reserves, riparian reserves, or environmentally fragile land [(Rutto & Odhiambo, 2017); (Vizzuality, 2022)]. County (2013) noted that illegal settlers cleared approximately 500 hectares of the indigenous forest in Kipkurere forest. In Uasin Gishu County, some of the potential forest areas that have been cleared of natural vegetation and converted to agricultural land include Timboroa and Nabkoi forests (Chebii, 2015). These forests have, however, been fragmented by commercial plantation forests mainly in the fertile areas using exotic species (Chebii, 2015). Apart from the danger of forest fires in Uasin Gishu County, selling the former EATEC farms to individuals had also reduced the proportion of the forest cover (County, 2013).

As stated earlier, gender distribution is very significant to forest conservation and management as each side of the gender divide is precisely suited for specific activities. In Uasin Gishu County, more women as compared to their male counterparts are actively engaged in Community Forest Association (CFA) (Achungo, 2015). Rotich et al. (2017) in their study also identified recent indications of a shift in societal norms, whereby women in Kapsaret had started taking over management roles of some of the farm activities from men. A wide range of reasons could explain this shift, but none of them could elaborate on whether women had some control over agroforestry trees existing on their farms. According to Rotich et al. (2017), men and women play different roles in the community hence in different ways hindering the availability and utilization of agroforestry trees (for instance, men might want to plant trees for poles and timber to support construction, while women may do it for wood fuel).

3.3 Forests in Elgeyo Marakwet County

This county hosts the second largest forest cover in Kenya of 37.6% and is home to two forest ecosystems and water towers, namely Kaptagat and Cherangany Hills (Cheruiyot, 2019). The forest cover in this count is mainly divided into natural indigenous (78185.08 Ha) and plantation (12611.5 Ha) forest types (Marakwet, 2018). The county's primary sources of household cooking energy are firewood, charcoal, and paraffin (Johnston et al., 2018) which have contributed to vegetation degradation. Murkomen (2019) clearly showed the relationship between climate change and deforestation in Embobut and Tirap forests. The county residents believe that forests are the source of rainfall that feeds many rivers in the county (Murkomen, 2019). High population growth is connected to the felling of trees on hills in the effort to create human settlements [(Cheruiyot, 2019), (Murkomen, 2019)]. Incidences of landlessness in this county have recently been limited to gazetted forests (principally Embobut, Kipkabus, and Chebara forests) with Embobut Forest harboring approximately 500 family squatters therein (Marakwet, 2018).

Some of the key forest products in the county consist of firewood, honey, timber, grass, pine gum, herbal medicine, tree-nursery soils, building materials, and pottery clay (Marakwet, 2018). These forest products are the main reasons for the overreliance by humans on forest resources in this county. A report by UNDP shows that deforestation in both Elgeyo Marakwet and West Pokot County has been contributing to increasing mudslides, floods, and landslides (UNDP, 2022). Several environmental challenges which propel forest degradation in Elgeyo Marakwet County include forest encroachment, deforestation, overgrazing, unlawful logging, forest fires, and the burning of charcoal, particularly along the escarpment and Kerio valley (Marakwet,

2018). Grazing and agricultural expansion, for instance, are the two most significant causes of deforestation in the Cherangany hills forest ecosystem (Rotich & Ojwang, 2021). According to Marakwet (2018), these anthropogenic problems have led to the destruction of watersheds thus bringing about a reduction in water flow and rising resource-based conflicts amongst the communities living downstream. This, therefore, calls for a relook into which human activities work for the best interest of both the people and the environment.

Women's roles and participation in the management and use of community forestry have lately been explored in several empirical and theoretical papers. Just like the other two counties, Elgeyo Marakwet County has a clear distinction concerning gender roles and responsibilities relating to the management, use, and access of forest resources. Elgeyo Marakwet County's gender inequality index (GII) is at 0.62 compared to the national average of 0.55 an indication that this county has a higher level of gender inequality above the national average (Marakwet, 2018). A study conducted in Elgeyo Marakwet County's Kapchemutwa Forest showed that men and young people relied on the forest for charcoal, timber, and poles whereas women generally got herbal medicine, firewood, and food from the same forest (Serem, 2016). Serem (2016) cited that knowledge on forest resources, climatic conditions, and cultural values also influenced the access, use, and management of forest resources. Livestock overgrazing in Kaptagat Forest particularly in newly planted areas was also mentioned as one of the factors that hindered the regeneration of the forest (Braitstein & Njenga, 2014). Braustein and Njenga (2014) further pointed out that women and children threatened the regeneration of Kaptagat Forest by harvesting young indigenous trees for firewood.

4. CONCLUSION AND RECOMMENDATION

As far as gender roles and responsibilities concerning the management of forest resources go, a lot still needs to be done to ensure the efficiency of integrated supervision of all the forest resources in these three counties. More women should be included in the process of decision-making. This will result in higher quality policies regarding forest resource management, positive economic outcomes and performances, and progressive policy agenda. Based on the available literature, there exists an undeniable trend about gender roles in the management of forest resources in all three counties. Studies show that male dominance in the management of forest resources could pose a challenge to their access and subsequent usage.

To promote gender equity in the utilization of forest resources and to ensure that women also benefit fully, this paper recommends several policies, technological and institutional interventions. Firstly, it recommends that women should be enabled to establish and strengthen existing associations. This will provide women with platforms to showcase their talents as well as to air and document their opinion about their perceived forest management best practices. Secondly, this paper proposes that women should be assisted to improve productivity and the marketing of products considered to be in women's field of expertise. This will not only be beneficial in the context of the value addition of other resources that may be derived from the forests such as honey and herbal medicines but also the correct pricing and the identification of markets of said products. Last but not least, it recommends the improvement of women's access to information by training more women extension staff, holding separate meetings for women farmers involved in agroforestry, and ensuring that women are fully represented in all activities. This will empower women by arming them with the necessary skillsets relevant to the sustainable management of this natural resource.

This paper suggests that the three counties should consolidate their effort to comanage forest resources that have transboundary/trans-county benefits. This will be cost-effective to each county that is involved. In addition, this study suggests that all three counties increase forest cover through the intensification of both agroforestry and afforestation. This would be quite beneficial particularly if both men and women participated in the planting of indigenous medicinal tree species. This approach will also aid in the rejuvenation and by extension the replenishment of key water catchment areas and water towers. These two activities will help in the much-needed boost toward a higher tree replanting rate, mainly in Uasin Gishu County.

The three county governments in association with the national government and other stakeholders should help the residents of these counties identify and use cheaper sustainable and environmentally friendly alternative fuel sources (such as solar energy) to replace firewood and charcoal. This will help a long way in the management of the carbon footprint by reduction of both deforestation and the emission of greenhouse gases. The efficiency and reliability of a cleaner source of energy will make work much easier for women as far as the search for fuel for domestic use is concerned.

Each community that relies on forest resources in all three counties should involve its residents (both men and women) in the management of forests at a local level. This approach will only be favorable if all the residents of these communities are subjected to equal opportunities to adequate training on how to sustainably manage the forest resources. The learning process should incorporate multifaceted teaching of important skill sets from both relevant traditional indigenous knowledge and through modern programs that seek to guide the management, access, and usage of these resources. The integrated approach will present opportunities that shall aid in controlling practices such as deforestation, overgrazing, and illicit logging within these forests through applied precision in afforestation and agroforestry.

REFERENCES

Achungo, T. O. (2015). Influence of plantation establishment and livelihood improvement scheme on forest cover: A case of Uasin Gishu County, Kenya.

Alliance, H. C. (2022). Water Catchment Areas (Watersheds) | Welcome to Hill Country Alliance. https://hillcountryalliance.org/our-work/water-resources/water-catchment-areas-watersheds/

Braitstein, P., & Njenga, M. (2014). Women, poverty and forest destruction: Despite sensitization womenfolk continue to cut indigenous trees for firewood. Miti. The Tree Business Magazine for Africa, 20-21.

Britannica. (2022). Forest | Definition, Ecology, Types, Trees, Examples, & Facts | Britannica. https://www.britannica.com/science/forest

Canada, N. R. (2017). Forest-ecosystem-products-services. Natural Resources Canada. https://www.nrcan.gc.ca/our-natural-resources/forests-and-forestry/sustainable-forest-management/forest-ecosystem-products-services/13177

Catchments. (2022). What is a catchment, and why should you care? Catchments.Ie. https://www.catchments.ie/catchment-i-care/

Centre, E. (2020, November 29). Names of Forests in Kenya. Elimu Centre. https://www.elimucentre.com/names-of-forests-in-kenya/

Centre, U. W. H. (2022). Sacred Mijikenda Kaya Forests. UNESCO World Heritage Centre. https://whc.unesco.org/en/list/1231/

Chazdon, R. L., Brancalion, P. H. S., Laestadius, L., Bennett-Curry, A., Buckingham, K., Kumar, C., Moll-Rocek, J., Vieira, I. C. G., & Wilson, S. J. (2016). When is a forest a forest? Forest concepts and definitions in the era of forest and landscape restoration. Ambio, 45(5), 538–550. https://doi.org/10.1007/s13280-016-0772-y

Chebii, J. K. (2015). Forest management and conservation in Kenya: A study of the role of law in the conservation of forest resources.

Cheboiwo, J. K., Mutta, D., Kiprop, J., & Gattama, S. (2018). Public private partnerships opportunities for forestry sector development in Kenya: Synthesis of primary and secondary production actors, and trade. Actors and Trade, 8(1), 47–69.

Cheruiyot, S. A. (2019). Forest Planning and Management for Human Development in Africa: A Case of Kenya.

Chiwona-Karltun, L., Kimanzu, N., Clendenning, J., Lodin, J. B., Ellingson, C., Lidestav, G., Mkwambisi, D., Mwangi, E., Nhantumbo, I., Ochieng, C., Petrokofsky, G., & Sartas, M. (2017). What is the evidence that gender affects access to and use of forest assets for food security? A systematic map protocol. Environmental Evidence, 6(1), 2. https://doi.org/10.1186/s13750-016-0080-9

Colfer, C. J. P. (2013). The gender box: A framework for analyzing gender roles in forest management (Vol. 82). CIFOR.

County Government of Nandi. (2018). County integrated development plan 2018-2023: Achieving sustainable and all-inclusive social economic transformation. County Government of Nandi, Kenya.

County Government of Uasin Gishu. (2018). COUNTY INTERGRATED DEVELOPMENT PLAN (CIDP) 2018-2022. County Government of Uasin Gishu.

County, U. G. (2013). Uasin Gishu county integrated development plan 2013-2018. Report Sept 2013.

Daily, B. (2020, December 27). Uasin Gishu community plants 23,000 trees in Timboroa forest. Business Daily. https://www.businessdailyafrica.com/bd/news/counties/uasin-gishu-community-plants-23-000-trees-in-timboroa-forest-2203146

Daily, B. (2021, July 26). Counties hold key to meeting 10pc forest cover goal by 2022. Business Daily. https://www.businessdailyafrica.com/bd/data-hub/counties-hold-key-to-meeting-10pc-forest-cover-goal-by-2022-3487402

Das, N. (2011). Women's dependence on forest and participation in forestry: A case study of joint forest management programme in West Bengal. Journal of Forest Economics, 17(1), 67–89.

EMCA. (2015). EMCA Act 2015 — Environmental Management and Coordination Act 2015 -. StuDocu. https://www.studocu.com/row/document/multimedia-university-of-kenya/chemistry/emca-act-2015-environmental-management-and-coordination-act-2015/9821324

FAO. (2015). Agroforestry. https://www.fao.org/forestry/agroforestry/80338/en/

FAO. (2020). Natural Forest Management. https://www.fao.org/forestry/sfm/85084/en/

20

FAO. (2022a). In more depth | SFM Toolbox | Food and Agriculture Organization of the United Nations. https://www.fao.org/sustainable-forest-management/toolbox/modules/gender-in-forestry/in-more-depth/en/

FAO. (2022b). The State of the World's Forests 2020. Www.Fao.Org. https://doi.org/10.4060/CA8642EN

Fashing, P. J., Forrestel, A., Scully, C., & Cords, M. (2004). Long-term tree population dynamics and their implications for the conservation of the Kakamega Forest, Kenya. Biodiversity & Conservation, 13(4), 753–771.

FCMA. (2016). No. 34 of 2016. http://kenyalaw.org:8181/exist/kenyalex/actview.xql?actid=No.%2034%20of%202016

FLEGT. (2022). What is illegal logging? | FLEGT. https://www.euflegt.efi.int/illegal-logging

Forest, K. (2021). Kenyaforests.org. https://www.kenyaforests.org/index.php/what-we-do/monitoring-of-water-towers

GEN. (2022). Gender and the Environment. Www.Genevaenvironmentnetwork.Org. https://www.genevaenvironmentnetwork.org/resources/updates/gender-and-the-environment/

Greenpeace. (2022). Solutions to Deforestation. Greenpeace USA. https://www.greenpeace.org/usa/forests/solutions-to-deforestation/

GroCycle. (2022). Agroforestry Ultimate Guide and Examples—GroCycle. Www.Grocycle.Com. https://grocycle.com/agroforestry-ultimate-guide/

IFPC. (2022). Environmental Benefits of Forests Archives · Idaho Forests Products Commission. https://www.idahoforests.org/forest-information-topic/environmental-benefits-of-forests/

ISSUU. (2015). North and South Nandi Forests Strategic Ecosystems Management Plan 2015 – 2040 by Nature Kenya Publications – Issuu. https://issuu.com/nature_kenya/docs/nandi_forests_strategic_plan_2015-2

Jacobson, M., & Smith, S. S. (2016). Sustainable Forestry. Penn State Extension. https://extension.psu.edu/sustainable-forestry

Jattan, P. S. (2003). Gender issues in participatory forest management in India. Gender Issues, 799, C1.

Johnston, S. F., Matare, D., Pettersen, D., Mumba, R., Pullanikkatil, D., Zachary, S., & Karimi, N. (2018). Kenya-Malawi Biomass Energy Project Summary Report.

Kagombe, J. (2015). North and South Nandi Forest forests strategic Ecosystem Management Plan 2015 -2040.

Kenya, L. O. (2013). The constitution of Kenya: 2010. Chief Registrar of the Judiciary.

Kenya. Ministry of Planning and National Development & Kenya. National Economic and Social Council. (2007). Kenya: Vision 2030. Government of the Republic of Kenya, Ministry of Planning and National Development and the National Economic and Social Council (NESC), Office of the President. https://books.google.co.ke/books?id=wZYnAQAAIAAJ

Kenya, T. (2013). Pathway to devolution, socio-economic development, equity and national unity. Second Medium Term Plan (MTP) Report, Government of the Republic of Kenya.

Kim, K. H., & Zabelina, D. L. (2011). Underachievement. In M. A. Runco & S. R. Pritzker (Eds.), Encyclopedia of Creativity (Second Edition) (pp. 503–508). Academic Press. https://doi.org/10.1016/B978-0-12-375038-9.00253-3

King-Okumu, C., Tsegai, D., Sanogo, D., Kiprop, J., Cheboiwo, J., Sarr, M. S., da Cunha, M. I., & Salman, M. (2021). How can we stop the slow-burning systemic fuse of loss and damage due to land degradation and drought in Africa? Current Opinion in Environmental Sustainability, 50, 289–302.

Kiptot, E. (2015). Gender roles, responsibilities, and spaces: Implications for agroforestry research and development in Africa. The International Forestry Review, 17, 11–21.

Kiptot, E., & Franzel, S. (2012). Gender and agroforestry in Africa: A review of women's participation. Agroforestry Systems, 84(1), 35–58. https://doi.org/10.1007/s10457-011-9419-y

KNA. (2019). Uasin Gishu County promotes Bamboo planting to increase forest cover – Kenya News Agency. https://www.kenyanews.go.ke/uasin-gishu-county-promotes-bamboo-planting-to-increase-forest-cover/

Koech, C. K. (2020). Household Factors Affecting the Implementation of Forest Conservation Strategies: A Case of South Nandi Forest, Nandi County, Kenya.

Open Journal of Social Sciences, 8(6), 125–144. https://doi.org/10.4236/jss.2020.86012

LLC, T. L. (2017, June 8). Forest Management—Importance. Turner Logging, LLC. https://turnerloggingllc.com/forest-management-important/

Maini, J. (1992). Sustainable development of forests. Unasylva, 43(169), 3–8.

Marakwet, C. G. of E. (2018). Elgeyo Marakwet County CIDP II (2018-2022). County Government of Elgeyo Marakwet.

Marin, A. B., & Kuriakose, A. T. (2017). Gender and sustainable forest management: Entry points for design and implementation. Climate Investment Funds Washington, DC.

Millennium ecosystem assessment, M. (2005). Ecosystems and human well-being (Vol. 5). Island press Washington, DC.

Mongabay. (2021). Kenya Forest Information and Data. https://rainforests.mongabay.com/deforestation/2000/Kenya.htm

Morara, O. G., & Kiptoo, S. J. (2018). Kenya's Water Towers; A Scenario Scrutiny of Njoro Sub Catchment, Eastern Mau Towers. 10.

Murkomen, L. (2019). Climate variability adaptation using fodder crops: A case study of Marakwet East Sub-county, Elgeyo–Marakwet County.

Mwangi, E., Meinzen-Dick, R., & Sun, Y. (2011). Gender and sustainable forest management in East Africa and Latin America. Ecology and Society, 16(1).

NEMA. (2022). National Environment Management Authority (NEMA)—Towards 10 percent forest cover.

https://www.nema.go.ke/index.php?option=com_content&view=article&id=30 6:towards-10-percent-tree-cover&catid=10&Itemid=462

Nhem, S., & Lee, Y. J. (2019). Women's participation and the gender perspective in sustainable forestry in Cambodia: Local perceptions and the context of forestry research. Forest Science and Technology, 15(3), 93–110. https://doi.org/10.1080/21580103.2019.1595174

Oregon Forest Resources Institute. (2022). Forest Benefits. https://oregonforests.org/forest-benefits

PEFC. (2022). Benefits of forests—PEFC - Programme for the Endorsement of Forest Certification. https://pefc.org/what-we-do/why-forests-are-important/the-benefits-of-forests

Peltorinne, P. (2004). The forest types of Kenya.

Phiri, A. T., Toure, H. M., Kipkogei, O., Traore, R., Afokpe, P. M., & Lamore, A. A. (2022). A review of gender inclusivity in agriculture and natural resources management under the changing climate in sub-Saharan Africa. Cogent Social Sciences, 8(1), 2024674.

Ros-Tonen, M. A., Reed, J., & Sunderland, T. (2018). From synergy to complexity: The trend toward integrated value chain and landscape governance. Environmental Management, 62(1), 1–14.

Rotich, B., & Ojwang, D. (2021). Trends and drivers of forest cover change in the Cherangany hills forest ecosystem, western Kenya. Global Ecology and Conservation, 30, e01755. https://doi.org/10.1016/j.gecco.2021.e01755

Rutto, G., & Odhiambo, K. (2017). Socio-economic importance of tree nurseries in eldoret municipality, Uasin Gishu County (Kenya). Africa Environmental Review Journal, 2(2), 146–154.

Schnell, S., Kleinn, C., & Ståhl, G. (2015). Monitoring trees outside forests: A review. Environmental Monitoring and Assessment, 187(9), 1–17.

Serem, M. J. (2016). INFLUENCE OF GENDER ON ACCESS, USE AND MANAGEMENT OF FOREST RESOURCES IN KAPCHEMUTWA FOREST, ELGEYO MARAKWET COUNTY, KENYA.

Sigu, G., Omenda, T., Ongugo, P., & Opiyo, A. (2000). Sacred Groves Institutions, Rule Enforcement and Impact on Forest Condition: The case of Ramogi Hill Forest Reserve, Kenya. Nairobi, Kenya, Kenya Forestry Research Institute.

Society, N. G. (2019). Deforestation | National Geographic Society. https://www.nationalgeographic.org/encyclopedia/deforestation/

Tanui, J., & Saina, C. (2015). The physical state of forest cover and landuse in Kenya–A case of Nandi Hills in Nandi County, Kenya. European Journal of Agricultural and Forestry Research, 3(3), 1–14.

Tong, R. (2012). Gender Roles. In R. Chadwick (Ed.), Encyclopedia of Applied Ethics (Second Edition) (pp. 399–406). Academic Press. https://doi.org/10.1016/B978-0-12-373932-2.00307-0

UN. (2022). Forests | Department of Economic and Social Affairs. https://sdgs.un.org/topics/forests

UNDP. (2022). Conserving forests to reduce landslides and flooding and fight climate change in Kenya's Elgeyo Marakwet Water Tower | Climate and Forests. https://www.climateandforests-undp.org/conserving-forests-reduce-landslides-and-flooding-and-fight-climate-change-kenya%E2%80%99s-elgeyo-marakwet

Vizzuality. (2022). Uasin Gishu, Kenya Deforestation Rates & Statistics | GFW. https://www.globalforestwatch.org/dashboards/country/KEN/44

WHO. (2022). Gender: Definitions. https://www.euro.who.int/en/health-topics/health-determinants/gender/gender-definitions

YOUR KNOWLEDGE HAS VALUE